This special book belongs to

_____

_____

_____

Copyright © Anna Cerridwen 2024

Published with Ingram Spark

First published 2024

ISBN: 978 106832760 5

All rights reserved. No part of this publication may be reproduced, stored in a retrieval system, or transmitted, in any form or by any means, electronic, mechanical, photocopying, recording or otherwise, without the prior permission of the publishers.

My stepdad is the best

Written by Anna Cerridwen

Illustrated by Natasha Poposka - de Bats

I love my stepdad;
he's good to me.

He makes me smile,
I'm happy as can be.

My stepdad loves me
and will always be there.

He gives hugs if I want them,
and oodles of care.

My stepdad can't fly;
he has no magic powers,

But I would pick him,
if stepdads were flowers.

He likes to play games,
to be silly and funny,

We kick balls outside
when it's nice and sunny.

If I fall, he puts a plaster on my knee.

He's patient and kind and loving to me.

He makes me laugh,
he jokes and he sings.

My stepdad teaches me
loads of new things.

He teaches me it
doesn't matter who won,

What's important is
to have lots of fun.

He gently brushes
my hair with a comb,

He brings lots of happiness
into our home.

He cooks yummy meals
and he washes my clothes,

Never shouts at me,
even when I'd hurt his nose!

If I've upset him
and he looks a bit sad,

I say sorry, we hug
and I stop feeling mad.

We sit down together
and read lots of books.

When in the kitchen,
we pretend to be cooks.

We have so much fun
when we visit the park,

Sometimes we pretend
he's a big, scary shark!

By the end of the day
when I am all mucky,

He runs me a bath
and I feel very lucky.

My stepdad is great,
the best I could wish for.

Someone who cares,
and who I adore.

I don't mind if he earns
many hundreds of pounds,

Whether he drives,
rides horses, or walks around.

He could look nothing like me,
be tall or small,

What he looks like
doesn't matter at all.

All that's important is
he really loves me.

I've got the best stepdad
there ever could be!

www.ingramcontent.com/pod-product-compliance
Lightning Source LLC
Chambersburg PA
CBHW041436010526
44118CB00002B/86